Mastering the RAG: A Practical Guide to Deploying

AI-Powered Data Retrieval and Generation in Your

Enterprise -ERP, SAP, SFDC

Contents

1. Introduction

The way we interact with data in enterprise

applications is on the cusp of a revolution. Enter the

Retrieval-Augmented Generation (RAG) pattern, a

powerful AI technique poised to transform how you access and utilize information within core systems like Oracle ERP, SAP, and Salesforce (SFDC).

1.1 What is the RAG Pattern?

Imagine a system that acts as your intelligent assistant within your

enterprise applications. The RAG pattern combines two key components:

1. **Retrieval:** This component acts like a super-powered search engine, digging deep into your enterprise data sources (ERP, SAP, SFDC) to find the most relevant information based on your query.

2. **Generation:** Here's where the magic happens. The retrieved data is fed into a Large Language Model (LLM), a powerful AI tool that can understand and process information like a human. The LLM then generates a response, like a report, summary, or even creative text formats tailored to your needs.

Think of RAG as a bridge – it connects your questions with the vast data reserves within your enterprise applications, presenting the information in a clear and actionable way.

1.2 Benefits of RAG for Enterprise Applications

The benefits of RAG for businesses are numerous:

- **Enhanced Efficiency:** No more sifting through endless reports or struggling with complex queries. RAG retrieves and analyzes data in a flash, saving you valuable time and effort.

- **Deeper Insights:** Gain a more comprehensive understanding of your data. RAG can generate insightful reports and summaries, helping you identify trends and make data-driven decisions with confidence.

- **Improved Automation:** Automate repetitive tasks like report generation and data analysis. RAG can free up your workforce to focus on higher-level strategic initiatives.

- **Increased Productivity:** Spend less time searching for information and more time taking action. RAG streamlines workflows and empowers employees to be more productive.

- **Enhanced User Experience:** RAG makes interacting with enterprise data more intuitive and user-friendly. Imagine a conversational interface where you can ask questions and receive clear, concise answers.

1.3 Use Cases for RAG in ERP, SAP, and SFDC

The potential applications of RAG are vast and can be tailored to specific needs within different enterprise systems:

- **Oracle ERP:** Generate financial reports with ease, analyze sales trends in real-time, and gain insights into inventory levels.

- **SAP:** Simplify customer relationship management, predict potential supply chain disruptions, and automate repetitive tasks in HR.

- **Salesforce (SFDC):** Generate personalized sales proposals, identify high-value leads, and automate sales forecasting with greater accuracy.

These are just a few examples. The possibilities with RAG are truly limitless, empowering businesses to unlock the full potential of their data and gain a significant competitive advantage.

2. Pre-Deployment Considerations: Laying the groundwork for a successful RAG implementation

Before diving into the exciting world of RAG deployment, there are some key factors to consider to ensure a smooth and successful process.

2.1 Identifying Data Sources and Compatibility

The foundation of any RAG system lies in its ability to access and retrieve relevant data. Here's a breakdown of the data sources you'll be working with in different enterprise applications:

- **2.1.1 Oracle ERP Data Sources:** Oracle ERP is a powerhouse for financial and operational data. RAG can tap into various modules like:
    - Financials: General Ledger, Accounts Payable/ Receivable
    - Inventory: Manage stock levels, track product movement
    - Sales: Analyze sales performance, generate reports on customer data

- **2.1.2 SAP Data Sources:** SAP offers a comprehensive suite of data encompassing various departments. RAG can connect to:

  - Sales & Distribution: Track orders, manage customer relationships

  - Human Resources: Access employee data, automate reports

  - Procurement: Streamline purchasing processes, gain insights into supplier performance

- **2.1.3 Salesforce Data Sources:** SFDC is a goldmine for customer-centric data. RAG can leverage:

  - Leads & Accounts: Identify high-value leads, manage customer information

- o Opportunities: Forecast sales more accurately, track deal progress

- o Activities & Tasks: Automate tasks, generate reports on sales team performance

Compatibility is key: Ensure your chosen RAG solution can seamlessly connect to your specific versions of Oracle ERP, SAP, and SFDC. This might involve working with APIs (Application Programming Interfaces) or establishing direct database access.

2.2 Choosing a Large Language Model (LLM) for your Needs

The LLM acts as the brain of your RAG system, interpreting retrieved data and generating human-like responses. Here's what to consider when choosing an LLM:

- **Domain-specific vs. General-purpose:** For optimal performance, consider an LLM pre-trained on data relevant to your industry and enterprise applications (e.g., finance for Oracle ERP, sales for SFDC). General-purpose LLMs can still be effective, but may require additional fine-tuning.

- **Accuracy and Explainability:** Choose an LLM known for its factual accuracy and ability to explain its reasoning behind generated text. This is crucial for ensuring trust and reliability in your RAG system.

- **Scalability and Performance:** Consider the volume of data you anticipate handling and choose an LLM that can handle it efficiently. Look for options that offer flexible deployment options (cloud-based vs. on-premise) to suit your needs.

2.3 Security Considerations for Enterprise Data Access

Security is paramount when dealing with sensitive enterprise data. Here are some key considerations:

- **Data Access Control:** Implement robust access controls to ensure only authorized users and processes can interact with your RAG system and access underlying data sources.

- **Data Encryption:** Encrypt data at rest and in transit to safeguard sensitive information from unauthorized access.

- **Auditing and Logging:** Maintain a comprehensive audit trail to track all interactions with the RAG system and data sources. This will help identify any potential security breaches.

By carefully considering these pre-deployment factors, you'll be well on your way to implementing a secure and effective RAG system that unlocks the true potential of your enterprise data.

3. Deployment Steps: Bringing Your RAG System to Life

Now that you've identified your data sources, chosen a powerful LLM, and prioritized security, it's time to delve into the exciting world of deployment! Here's a step-by-step breakdown of the process:

3.1 Setting Up the Retrieval Component: The Data Fetching Powerhouse

The retrieval component acts as the bridge between your RAG system and your enterprise applications. It's responsible for understanding your queries and efficiently retrieving the most relevant data.

- **3.1.1 Connecting RAG to Enterprise Applications (APIs, Database Access):** There are two main ways to connect RAG to your applications:

- APIs (Application Programming Interfaces): Many enterprise applications offer APIs that provide programmatic access to data. Your RAG system can leverage these APIs to interact and retrieve information. This is often the preferred method due to its ease of use and security features.

- Direct Database Access: For situations where APIs aren't available, RAG may be able to connect directly to your application's database. This approach requires in-depth knowledge of the database schema and may involve additional security considerations. *Deciding between APIs and direct database access will depend on the specific capabilities of your chosen RAG solution and your enterprise applications.*

- **3.1.2 Data Preprocessing and Indexing for Search:** Once the connection is established, the retrieved data needs some preparation before it's fed to the LLM. This preprocessing involves tasks like:

  - **Cleaning and Formatting:** Ensure data consistency by removing errors and standardizing formats.

- o **Normalization:** Structure the data in a way that facilitates efficient searching and retrieval.

- o **Indexing:** Create searchable indexes of the data to allow for lightning-fast retrieval based on user queries.

By effectively setting up the retrieval component, you're laying the groundwork for accurate and efficient data access within your RAG system.

3.2 Integrating the LLM Component: The Brains Behind the Operation

The LLM component is the heart of RAG, transforming retrieved data into insightful responses. Here's what you need to consider during integration:

- **3.2.1 Choosing a Platform for LLM Integration (Cloud-based vs. On-premise):** There are two main deployment options for your LLM:
  - **Cloud-based:** Cloud platforms offer a readily available and scalable solution. They handle infrastructure management, allowing you to focus on configuration and fine-tuning. However, cloud solutions may raise security concerns for some businesses with highly sensitive data.

- o **On-premise:** This approach gives you complete control over the LLM and your data. However, it requires significant investment in hardware, software, and expertise to manage the infrastructure.

The choice between cloud-based and on-premise deployment depends on your specific security requirements, budget, and technical expertise.

- **3.2.2 Fine-tuning the LLM for Enterprise Domain and Terminology:** While pre-trained LLMs offer a strong foundation, fine-tuning can significantly enhance their performance within your specific domain. This involves exposing the LLM to large amounts of text data relevant to your industry and enterprise applications (e.g., financial reports for Oracle ERP). By understanding your specific terminology and data structures, the LLM can generate more accurate and relevant responses to user queries.

3.3 Building the User Interface (UI) or Chatbot Interface: The Bridge Between You and Your Data

The final step is creating a user-friendly interface for interacting with your RAG system. This can be:

- **A Traditional User Interface (UI):** Design a user interface that allows users to enter their queries and view the generated responses in a clear and organized manner. This could be a web application or a dedicated desktop application.

- **A Chatbot Interface:** For a more conversational experience, consider building a chatbot interface. Users can interact with the RAG system through natural language queries, mimicking a chat conversation. This can be particularly user-friendly for mobile access.

Remember, the key is to ensure your chosen interface is intuitive and easy to navigate for all users within your organization.

By following these detailed steps, you'll successfully deploy a robust RAG system that empowers your workforce to unlock the true potential of your enterprise data.

4. Testing and Monitoring: Ensuring Your RAG

System Fires on All Cylinders

You've meticulously built your RAG system, but before unleashing it on the world, it's crucial to ensure it performs as expected. Here's what you need to do to fine-tune and monitor your RAG system for optimal results.

4.1 Evaluating RAG Performance on Sample Queries

Just like testing any new system, evaluating your RAG's performance is essential. Here's how to approach it:

- **Develop a Test Suite:** Create a set of sample queries that represent the types of questions users are likely to ask. These queries should cover various functionalities and data sources within your enterprise applications (ERP, SAP, SFDC).

- **Test, Analyze, Refine:** Run these sample queries through your RAG system and assess the generated responses. Are they accurate, relevant, and complete? If not, identify areas for improvement. This might involve fine-tuning the retrieval component or the LLM for better query understanding.

- **Iterate and Enhance:** Continuously refine your test suite as you gather user feedback and identify new use cases. This iterative process ensures your RAG system remains optimized for real-world scenarios.

4.2 Monitoring for Accuracy, Bias, and Explainability

Even the most sophisticated AI systems can exhibit

biases or generate inaccurate outputs. Here's how to

maintain vigilance:

- **Accuracy Monitoring:** Continuously monitor the

  accuracy of the information retrieved and

  presented by your RAG system. You can achieve

  this through manual review or by setting up

  automated data validation checks.

- **Bias Detection and Mitigation:** Be aware of

  potential biases within your data sources or the

  LLM itself. Regularly assess the RAG's outputs

  for signs of bias and take corrective measures

like retraining the LLM with more balanced datasets.

- **Explainability and Transparency:** It's crucial to understand the reasoning behind the LLM's generated responses. Look for RAG solutions that offer some level of explainability, allowing you to identify the data sources and rationale used to create the outputs. This transparency builds trust in your RAG system.

4.3 User Feedback and Iteration

The best way to ensure your RAG system meets user needs is to involve them in the process:

- **Gather User Feedback:** Actively solicit feedback from users who interact with your RAG system. Ask them about its ease of use, the quality of the generated responses, and any suggestions for improvement.

- **Iterate Based on Feedback:** Don't treat deployment as a one-time event. Use the valuable insights gleaned from user feedback to continuously iterate and improve your RAG system. This might involve adjusting the user interface, refining the retrieval component, or fine-tuning the LLM for better response generation.

By implementing a robust testing and monitoring strategy, you can ensure your RAG system delivers accurate, unbiased, and user-friendly results. Remember, continuous improvement is key to maximizing the value of your RAG system for your organization.

Chapter: Integrating AI-Powered Retrieval-Augmented Generation with ERP Systems

In the evolving landscape of enterprise solutions, Retrieval-Augmented Generation (RAG) is revolutionizing how data is accessed, interpreted, and utilized. ERP systems like SAP, Oracle, and Microsoft Dynamics are the backbone of enterprise operations, hosting vast troves of structured and unstructured data. With the incorporation of RAG, enterprises can unlock actionable insights from their ERP systems, enhancing decision-making processes, streamlining workflows, and optimizing resource allocation.

A cornerstone of deploying RAG within ERP systems lies in its ability to bridge the gap between static databases and dynamic query-based insights. Traditional ERP solutions rely on predefined schemas and rigid data structures. However, with RAG,

enterprises can enable natural language interfaces,

allowing users to extract, process, and generate

actionable insights from disparate datasets in real

time.

RAG integrates a powerful information retrieval

module with generative AI, enabling seamless

interaction with the vast, fragmented datasets typical

in ERP systems. Imagine a supply chain manager

querying the ERP system to determine delays in

shipments: instead of manually sifting through

logistics, procurement, and vendor communication

modules, RAG processes the query, retrieves the

relevant data points, and generates a concise, actionable report.

To deploy RAG in ERP environments, enterprises must address several challenges:

1. **Data Access and Integration**: ERP systems host data in siloed environments, with varying levels of access and permissions. Implementing RAG necessitates a robust data integration pipeline, ensuring seamless access to real-time data while adhering to security and compliance protocols.

2. **Custom Query Understanding**: Each enterprise has unique workflows, terminologies, and datasets. RAG systems must be tailored to understand domain-specific language, ensuring

that the generative responses align with the enterprise's operational context.

3. **Performance Optimization**: ERP systems are mission-critical. Any AI-powered augmentation, like RAG, must operate efficiently without straining existing infrastructure. Fine-tuning retrieval and generation models, leveraging caching mechanisms, and deploying inference optimizations are essential to maintaining system performance.

Through advanced embeddings and fine-tuning, RAG models can cater to ERP-specific use cases, such as predictive maintenance, financial forecasting, and customer behavior analysis. The integration of SAP

HANA with OpenAI models or Salesforce Einstein GPT demonstrates the potential of such synergy, offering intelligent insights directly embedded into ERP workflows.

Chapter: Enhancing SAP Analytics with RAG for Real-Time Insights

SAP systems, renowned for their comprehensive enterprise solutions, often serve as repositories of massive datasets. From inventory records to financial statements, these systems enable organizations to maintain operational control. However, deriving actionable insights from SAP's vast dataset is a challenge RAG excels at addressing.

By layering RAG over SAP, organizations can enable:

- **Contextualized Data Retrieval**: Instead of manually extracting data through SAP Query or ABAP, users can leverage natural language prompts to retrieve precise datasets. For example, querying, *"What is the trend in Q3 inventory levels across regions?"* prompts the RAG system to fetch relevant SAP data and generate a meaningful response.

- **Automated Report Generation**: SAP environments often require extensive manual effort to consolidate reports. With RAG, enterprises can automate this process. The generative aspect simplifies complex data interpretations, producing narratives or visualizations that convey key insights.

- **Predictive Analytics with Real-Time Feedback**: RAG can integrate with SAP's predictive analytics capabilities. For instance, combining historical sales data with current market trends enables predictive insights, such as anticipating supply shortages or identifying high-risk inventory items.

Deploying RAG in SAP environments requires strategic customization:

- **Embedding Strategy**: Pre-trained embeddings can be fine-tuned to align with SAP's proprietary data structures, ensuring retrieval accuracy.
- **Integration with SAP Cloud Platform**: The SAP Cloud Platform serves as an ideal foundation for

integrating RAG models, leveraging its APIs and extensibility.

Real-world applications demonstrate the transformative potential. A leading automotive manufacturer integrated RAG into their SAP S/4HANA system to enhance demand planning. This enabled dynamic adjustments to production schedules based on real-time insights into supply chain fluctuations and customer demands, leading to cost savings and improved delivery timelines.

Chapter: Advanced SFDC Implementations with RAG for Sales and Customer Success

Salesforce (SFDC) remains a pioneer in customer relationship management (CRM). However, the sheer volume of customer interactions, sales records, and service requests often overwhelms traditional query-based systems. RAG offers a game-changing paradigm for Salesforce users, blending retrieval precision with AI-powered narrative generation.

Key benefits of integrating RAG with Salesforce include:

- **Personalized Customer Interactions**: RAG empowers sales and support teams to fetch customer-specific insights instantly. When a customer reaches out, agents can prompt the system for a detailed account of their history, recent transactions, and sentiment analysis.

- **Lead Prioritization and Management**: By synthesizing data from Salesforce's Einstein Analytics, RAG can identify high-priority leads, score them dynamically, and recommend personalized outreach strategies.

- **Dynamic Playbook Recommendations**: Generative AI can create actionable playbooks for sales teams based on real-time market analysis and historical CRM data. This ensures that sales representatives are equipped with strategies tailored to each lead.

Deploying RAG within Salesforce involves strategic decisions:

- **Apex and Lightning Integration**: Leveraging Salesforce's Apex language and Lightning Platform ensures seamless embedding of RAG modules.

- **Real-Time Data Syncing**: Synchronizing with Salesforce objects and external data sources requires robust API orchestration to deliver real-time insights.

Case studies highlight RAG's impact. A financial services company utilized RAG to streamline its customer success operations. By analyzing historical data, the RAG system identified patterns of churn and provided actionable recommendations to mitigate risks, leading to a 15% increase in customer retention.

Chapter: Securing RAG Deployments in Enterprise Systems

The integration of RAG into enterprise systems introduces challenges beyond technical implementation, particularly around data security and compliance. Given the sensitive nature of ERP, SAP, and Salesforce data, securing RAG deployments is paramount.

Core considerations for secure RAG deployment include:

- **Data Encryption and Access Control**: Ensure that all data retrieval and generation processes are encrypted end-to-end. Fine-grained access controls should be implemented, allowing only authorized personnel to access specific datasets.

- **Audit Trails and Transparency**: Deploying RAG systems with integrated logging mechanisms ensures every query and response is traceable. This enhances accountability and simplifies compliance reporting.

- **Model Privacy**: Generative models often retain some training data representations, leading to potential data leakage. Techniques such as differential privacy, secure enclaves, and federated learning are critical for mitigating such risks.

- **Compliance with Industry Standards**: Adhering to GDPR, CCPA, HIPAA, and other regulations ensures that RAG deployments respect data privacy and legal frameworks.

Case studies from industries such as healthcare and finance emphasize the necessity of secure RAG systems. A healthcare provider integrated RAG to streamline patient data access while ensuring compliance with HIPAA regulations. Secure architectures, including isolated inference environments and encrypted communication protocols, were essential for this deployment.

Chapter: Scaling RAG Across Enterprise Workflows

Scalability is a critical concern when deploying RAG in enterprise environments. Whether for ERP, SAP, or Salesforce systems, organizations must ensure that the RAG solution can handle the growing complexity and volume of enterprise data.

Strategies for scalable RAG deployment include:

- **Distributed Retrieval Architectures**: Implementing distributed systems ensures efficient handling of large datasets. Techniques such as sharding and caching can significantly enhance retrieval speeds.

- **Generative Model Optimization**: Large language models can be computationally intensive. Optimizations like parameter quantization, pruning, and fine-tuning on smaller datasets reduce computational overhead while preserving accuracy.

- **Pipeline Automation**: Integrating RAG with CI/CD pipelines enables dynamic updates to retrieval and generation modules. This ensures that the RAG system evolves with changing enterprise needs.

- **Cost Management**: Deploying RAG across enterprise-scale systems requires cost-efficient solutions. Leveraging serverless architectures, spot instances, and energy-efficient hardware minimizes deployment costs without compromising performance.

Scalable RAG systems can transform industries. A global retail chain integrated RAG into their ERP system to manage inventory and forecast demand across thousands of stores. The scalable architecture allowed real-time insights into inventory levels, enabling predictive restocking and reducing overhead costs.

Chapter: Advanced Query Optimization in RAG for Enterprise Systems

Query optimization is critical for ensuring that Retrieval-Augmented Generation (RAG) systems deliver accurate, relevant, and timely responses in enterprise environments. Traditional data retrieval methods often suffer from inefficiencies when handling complex queries or massive datasets. RAG, when fine-tuned for advanced query optimization, can significantly enhance performance and accuracy.

Key areas of focus for query optimization in RAG include:

- **Semantic Search Techniques**: Leveraging advanced embeddings, such as those from BERT or OpenAI models, ensures that queries are matched with the most contextually relevant data. Unlike keyword-based search, semantic search captures the intent behind queries, making retrieval more effective.

- **Query Preprocessing**: Enterprises often deal with unstructured or ambiguous queries. Preprocessing, such as entity recognition and disambiguation, ensures that queries are well-structured before retrieval begins.

- **Dynamic Query Rewriting**: RAG systems can rewrite queries on the fly, breaking down complex inputs into simpler sub-queries. This modular approach improves retrieval accuracy and aligns with multi-hop reasoning workflows.

- **Caching Frequently Accessed Data**: Implementing a caching mechanism for frequently queried datasets reduces response times and lowers computational overhead.

Real-world applications demonstrate the importance of optimization. A global logistics provider integrated RAG with its ERP system to streamline shipment tracking. By optimizing query preprocessing and enabling semantic search, the company reduced response times for customer inquiries by 40%, significantly improving satisfaction levels.

Chapter: Fine-Tuning RAG Models for Domain-Specific Applications

RAG's performance hinges on its ability to understand domain-specific terminologies, workflows, and data structures. Fine-tuning is the cornerstone of achieving this level of specialization, enabling enterprises to adapt generic RAG models to their unique operational contexts.

Key techniques for fine-tuning RAG models include:

- **Domain-Specific Dataset Preparation**: Curating and preprocessing datasets that reflect the language and structure of a specific domain is crucial. For instance, fine-tuning for healthcare applications requires datasets rich in medical terminologies and patient interaction logs.

- **Knowledge Injection**: Incorporating structured knowledge, such as ontologies or taxonomies, enhances the model's contextual understanding. For example, integrating financial regulations into a RAG model for banking applications ensures compliance-aware responses.

- **Transfer Learning**: Starting with pre-trained models and fine-tuning them on domain-specific datasets minimizes training time and computational resources while achieving high accuracy.

- **Evaluation and Iteration**: Fine-tuned models require rigorous evaluation against domain-specific benchmarks. Iterative retraining based on feedback loops ensures continual improvement.

A multinational law firm successfully fine-tuned RAG for legal document analysis. The model was trained on case law, legal contracts, and regulations, enabling attorneys to extract relevant precedents and summaries instantly, significantly reducing research time.

Chapter: Implementing Feedback Loops for Continuous Improvement in RAG

One of the most significant advantages of RAG systems is their ability to learn and adapt over time through feedback loops. Enterprises that implement robust feedback mechanisms can ensure that their RAG solutions remain accurate, relevant, and aligned with evolving business needs.

Key components of feedback loops in RAG include:

- **Explicit User Feedback**: Allowing users to rate responses provides direct input for retraining and refinement. For instance, a sales team using RAG in Salesforce can flag irrelevant or inaccurate insights, feeding this data back into the system.

- **Implicit Feedback Mechanisms**: Monitoring user behavior, such as query reformulations or time spent reviewing responses, offers valuable insights into system performance without requiring explicit feedback.

- **Reinforcement Learning**: Feedback can be used to train RAG systems using reinforcement learning techniques. This approach rewards accurate and helpful responses, gradually improving performance over time.

- **Anomaly Detection and Correction**: RAG systems should be equipped to identify anomalies, such as inconsistent retrievals or inappropriate generative outputs, and self-correct based on feedback loops.

An enterprise in the retail sector deployed RAG to assist customer service teams. By integrating feedback loops, the system improved its ability to address customer queries, achieving a 30% reduction in escalations within six months of deployment.

Chapter: Multi-Language Support in RAG for Global Enterprises

Global enterprises often operate in multilingual environments, necessitating RAG systems capable of retrieving and generating insights across various languages. Implementing multi-language support enhances accessibility, user satisfaction, and operational efficiency.

Key strategies for enabling multi-language support in RAG include:

- **Cross-Lingual Retrieval Models**: Leveraging models like mBERT or XLM-R ensures effective retrieval across languages. These models map queries and documents to a shared semantic space, enabling cross-lingual matching.

- **Language-Specific Fine-Tuning**: Generative capabilities require fine-tuning on language-specific datasets to ensure fluency, cultural appropriateness, and contextual accuracy.

- **Real-Time Translation Integration**: Combining RAG with translation APIs, such as AWS Translate or Google Translate, facilitates seamless interaction in environments with diverse language requirements.

- **Evaluation Metrics for Multilingual Outputs**: Enterprises must develop robust evaluation frameworks, such as BLEU or METEOR scores, to measure the quality of multilingual generative outputs.

A global manufacturing firm implemented multilingual RAG to support its international supply chain operations. By enabling cross-lingual query capabilities, the firm ensured that suppliers, distributors, and internal teams across continents could access consistent insights, fostering smoother collaboration.

Chapter: RAG-Driven Decision Intelligence for Enterprise Leaders

Decision intelligence is a critical area where RAG can drive transformative change. By combining real-time data retrieval with AI-powered analysis and narrative generation, RAG systems provide enterprise leaders with actionable insights to guide strategic decision-making.

Key applications of RAG in decision intelligence include:

- **Scenario Analysis**: RAG can retrieve historical data, simulate potential outcomes, and generate comprehensive reports for decision-makers. For example, during a merger, RAG can provide detailed analyses of financial data, workforce alignment, and regulatory compliance risks.

- **KPI Monitoring and Insights**: By integrating with ERP systems, RAG can track key performance indicators in real time, flag anomalies, and suggest corrective actions.

- **Automated Briefings**: Generative capabilities enable RAG to produce daily or weekly executive briefings, summarizing critical events, trends, and recommendations.

- **What-If Analysis**: Leaders can pose hypothetical scenarios, and RAG systems can retrieve relevant data, generate insights, and outline potential impacts.

A telecommunications giant utilized RAG to optimize its decision-making processes. The system provided real-time analyses of customer churn, network performance, and market trends, empowering leadership to make data-driven decisions that boosted profitability by 12% within a year.

5. Advanced Considerations: Taking Your RAG System to the Next Level

While we've covered the core functionalities of deploying a RAG system, here are some advanced considerations to unlock its full potential within your enterprise, especially for large-scale deployments:

5.1 Multi-lingual Support for Global Enterprises

If your organization operates globally, you might consider incorporating multi-lingual support into your RAG system. This would allow users to interact with the system and receive responses in their preferred language. Here's how to approach it:

- **Multilingual LLM Integration:** Explore LLMs that are pre-trained on multiple languages relevant to your global workforce. This would enable the system to understand and respond to queries across different languages.

- **Language Detection and Routing:** Implement functionalities within the retrieval component to automatically detect the user's language and route the query to the appropriate LLM.

By incorporating multi-lingual support, you can empower your global workforce to leverage the power of RAG regardless of their location or native language.

5.2 Integrating with Existing Knowledge Management Systems

Your organization likely has a wealth of existing knowledge stored in various knowledge management systems (KMS) like wikis, document repositories, or internal FAQs. Integrating RAG with these systems can unlock a new level of information accessibility:

- **Unified Search:** Allow users to search across both the RAG system's data sources and your existing KMS through a single interface. This eliminates the need to switch between different platforms to find the information they need.

- **Contextual Enrichment:** The RAG system can leverage information from your KMS to provide richer and more informative responses to user queries. For example, when a user asks a question about a specific product, the RAG system could not only retrieve relevant data from ERP but also pull up related user manuals or troubleshooting guides from the KMS.

This integration creates a more comprehensive information ecosystem within your organization, empowering users to find the knowledge they need quickly and efficiently.

5.3 Scalability and Performance Optimization

As your organization grows and the volume of data managed by your RAG system increases, ensuring scalability and optimal performance becomes crucial. Here are some strategies to consider:

- **Cloud-based Infrastructure:** For large-scale deployments, leveraging cloud-based infrastructure for your LLM and retrieval components can offer significant advantages.

Cloud platforms provide inherent scalability, allowing you to easily adjust resources based on your evolving needs.

- **Data Partitioning:** For very large datasets, consider partitioning your data based on specific criteria (e.g., department, product line). This can improve search efficiency and retrieval times within the RAG system.

- **Performance Monitoring and Optimization:** Continuously monitor the performance of your RAG system. Identify bottlenecks and implement optimizations to ensure smooth operation even with growing data volumes.

By proactively addressing scalability and performance, you can ensure your RAG system remains a reliable and valuable tool for your organization well into the future.

Leveraging RAG for End-to-End ERP Process Optimization

In large enterprises, ERP systems form the backbone of operational management. Integrating Retrieval-Augmented Generation (RAG) into these systems allows for the automation of complex processes, such as inventory management, production planning, and financial reconciliation. This chapter explores how RAG can be used to optimize end-to-end processes in ERP environments by enabling real-time decision-making and reducing manual intervention.

Key topics include:

- Automating data retrieval and report generation across ERP modules.

- Enhancing inventory management through predictive insights.

- Real-time production scheduling based on dynamic data retrieval.

- Streamlining financial processes, including audits and compliance checks.

- Case studies of enterprises achieving significant efficiency gains.

Transforming Customer Experience with RAG-Enhanced CRM Systems

Customer Relationship Management (CRM) systems are pivotal for delivering personalized experiences. With RAG, organizations can take CRM capabilities to the next level by generating actionable insights, personalized recommendations, and automated responses. This chapter details how enterprises are embedding RAG into CRM platforms like Salesforce, Dynamics 365, and HubSpot to revolutionize customer interactions.

Highlights:

- Retrieving and analyzing customer sentiment from diverse data sources.
- Automating responses to customer inquiries with high accuracy.

- Generating tailored marketing campaigns using retrieved and synthesized data.

- Enhancing lead scoring and prioritization for sales teams.

- Real-world examples of RAG-driven CRM transformations.

Accelerating Supply Chain Resilience with RAG

Global supply chains are more complex than ever, and disruptions can significantly impact business operations. This chapter focuses on how RAG systems enable enterprises to navigate supply chain challenges by retrieving critical information from contracts, logistics data, and market reports. It also covers how generative capabilities provide actionable

recommendations for minimizing risks.

Core topics:

- Real-time retrieval of supplier and logistics data

  for contingency planning.

- Forecasting demand and inventory needs with

  RAG insights.

- Automated generation of risk mitigation

  strategies during disruptions.

- Integrating RAG with supply chain management

  platforms like SAP SCM and Oracle SCM Cloud.

- Examples of improved supply chain resilience

  through RAG deployment.

Enhancing Compliance and Risk Management with RAG

Compliance is a critical function in highly regulated industries like finance, healthcare, and manufacturing. RAG systems simplify the process of monitoring, auditing, and reporting compliance by retrieving relevant regulations and generating insights. This chapter delves into the use of RAG for maintaining regulatory adherence and mitigating operational risks.

Key areas covered:

- Retrieving and summarizing regulatory changes from global databases.
- Automating compliance checks within ERP and financial systems.

- Identifying and mitigating risks using generative risk models.

- Leveraging RAG for audit preparation and reporting.

- Industry case studies on successful compliance implementations.

Revolutionizing Data-Driven Decision Making with RAG

Decision-making in enterprises often requires analyzing vast amounts of structured and unstructured data. This chapter explains how RAG systems can bridge the gap between data retrieval and actionable insights, enabling leadership to make faster, more informed decisions. It also examines how RAG integrates with business intelligence (BI) tools to enhance analytical capabilities.

Discussion points include:

- Combining RAG with BI tools like Power BI and Tableau.
- Retrieving multi-source data for comprehensive business analysis.
- Generating executive summaries and strategic recommendations.
- Deploying RAG systems for cross-departmental decision alignment.

- Examples of RAG-driven decisions yielding measurable business outcomes.

Case Study: Enhancing Customer Support with RAG in a Global Retail Chain

Background

A global retail chain faced challenges in managing customer queries across its multilingual customer support centers. Despite having a centralized knowledge base, agents often struggled to retrieve relevant information quickly, leading to increased call

durations and lower customer satisfaction.

Implementation

The company integrated a Retrieval-Augmented

Generation (RAG) system with its existing CRM and

knowledge base. The RAG solution was fine-tuned

with data from past interactions, FAQs, and product

manuals. For multilingual support, the system

incorporated mBERT for cross-lingual retrieval and

AWS Translate for on-the-fly translation.

Key implementation steps included:

1. **Data Integration**: Migrating existing knowledge

   base content into the RAG architecture.

2. **Agent Training**: Educating support teams to interact with the AI system effectively.

3. **Real-Time Feedback**: Adding mechanisms for agents to flag inaccurate responses.

Outcomes

The deployment reduced average call handling time by 30% and improved first-call resolution rates by 25%. Agents reported higher efficiency, and customer satisfaction scores rose by 20%. The multilingual capability allowed the company to unify support teams across regions, further cutting costs.

Lessons Learned

- A well-prepared knowledge base is critical for RAG's success.

- Integrating real-time feedback loops enhances accuracy over time.

- Multilingual support can transform global operations with minimal additional overhead.

Case Study: Accelerating Research and Development in a Pharmaceutical Company

Background

A pharmaceutical company needed to accelerate its R&D efforts by quickly analyzing large volumes of research papers, clinical trial data, and patents. Traditional methods involved manual data retrieval and summarization, which were time-consuming and prone to errors.

Implementation

The company deployed a RAG system tailored for scientific literature retrieval and summarization. It fine-tuned a pre-trained GPT model using domain-specific datasets, including PubMed articles and proprietary trial data. To ensure compliance, the system integrated with existing security and data governance frameworks.

Steps taken:

1. **Fine-Tuning**: Training the model on scientific datasets.

2. **Customization**: Adding domain-specific prompts for generating concise research summaries.

3. **Integration**: Embedding the RAG system into the company's internal R&D portal.

Outcomes

The RAG system reduced literature review times by 40% and enabled researchers to identify relevant studies faster. It also highlighted potential drug interactions and compliance risks, improving decision-making. The company estimated savings of $2 million annually in operational costs.

Lessons Learned

- Domain-specific fine-tuning maximizes RAG's effectiveness.
- Compliance integration is non-negotiable in regulated industries.

- AI systems can significantly shorten R&D cycles, giving firms a competitive edge.

Case Study: Optimizing Supply Chain Operations for a Manufacturing Giant

Background

A multinational manufacturing firm struggled with inefficiencies in its supply chain operations. Delays in identifying bottlenecks and retrieving supplier information led to increased costs and missed deadlines.

Implementation

The company implemented a RAG-powered solution integrated with its ERP and supplier databases. It used a combination of vector-based retrieval and generative AI to provide insights into supplier performance, inventory levels, and shipping delays.

Key steps:

1. **Data Unification**: Consolidating supply chain data from disparate systems.
2. **Real-Time Monitoring**: Setting up triggers for RAG to notify managers about delays or anomalies.

3. **Scenario Analysis**: Enabling "what-if" analyses to predict the impact of decisions.

Outcomes

The system reduced supply chain delays by 15% and improved supplier selection processes. Real-time insights helped managers address potential disruptions proactively, saving the company an estimated $5 million annually.

Lessons Learned

- Real-time data retrieval and analysis are invaluable for dynamic operations.
- Integrating RAG with legacy systems requires careful planning but yields significant ROI.

- Predictive capabilities empower better decision-making at all levels.

Case Study: Enhancing Sales Forecasting in a SaaS Company

Background

A SaaS company needed better sales forecasting to

allocate resources effectively and identify growth opportunities. Manual processes based on spreadsheets and disparate CRM data often led to inaccurate forecasts.

Implementation

The company integrated a RAG system with Salesforce and other CRM tools. The system retrieved historical sales data, customer interactions, and market trends while generating insights into pipeline health and revenue projections.

Steps included:

1. **Data Preprocessing**: Cleaning and normalizing CRM data.

2. **Generative Insights**: Training the model to generate narratives explaining forecast trends.

3. **Visualization**: Embedding outputs into dashboards for easy interpretation.

Outcomes

The RAG system improved forecasting accuracy by 25% and provided actionable insights that boosted sales performance. Sales teams appreciated the automated generation of pipeline reports, which freed up time for client engagement.

Lessons Learned

- Combining retrieval with generative capabilities provides both data and context.

- Accurate sales forecasting depends on high-quality input data.

- Automated narratives enhance decision-making and team alignment.

Case Study: Enabling Real-Time Compliance Monitoring in Financial Services

Background

A financial services firm faced challenges in

maintaining compliance with constantly evolving

regulations. Manually monitoring regulatory changes

and auditing transactions was resource-intensive and

error-prone.

Implementation

The firm implemented a RAG solution that retrieved

regulatory updates and generated compliance

summaries. It integrated with transaction monitoring

systems to flag potential violations in real-time.

Key steps:

1. **Regulatory Dataset Integration**: Aggregating

   data from global regulatory bodies.

2. **Custom Prompts**: Crafting prompts to identify

   compliance risks.

3. **Audit Trails**: Generating detailed reports for regulators and internal audits.

Outcomes

The system reduced compliance monitoring costs by 30% and significantly minimized the risk of non-compliance penalties. Real-time insights enabled proactive adjustments to policies and processes.

Lessons Learned

- Proactive compliance monitoring prevents costly penalties.
- RAG systems excel in dynamic, high-risk environments.
- Customization is essential to address industry-specific regulations.

Case Study: Improving Supplier Management in an ERP System

Background

A global electronics manufacturer faced difficulties managing its supplier network within its ERP system.

Supplier contracts, performance metrics, and compliance records were scattered across multiple systems, causing delays in decision-making and increasing procurement risks.

Implementation

The company deployed a RAG (Retrieval-Augmented Generation) system integrated with its existing SAP ERP. The system retrieved supplier-specific data from contracts, performance reviews, and compliance records while generating reports on supplier risks and opportunities.

Key steps:

1. **Data Consolidation**: Migrating fragmented supplier data into a centralized repository compatible with RAG.

2. **RAG Integration**: Customizing the system to pull relevant supplier metrics and generate actionable insights.

3. **Automated Reporting**: Creating weekly and monthly reports to track supplier KPIs.

Outcomes

The RAG system improved supplier evaluation processes, reducing decision-making time by 40%. The company reported a 15% decrease in procurement costs through better contract negotiation enabled by quick access to supplier data.

Lessons Learned

- Data centralization is crucial for RAG's effectiveness in ERP systems.

- Automated insights significantly enhance procurement efficiency.

- Customizing RAG to specific use cases ensures better ROI.

Case Study: Streamlining HR Operations with RAG in SAP SuccessFactors

Background

A multinational corporation struggled with slow HR processes, including onboarding, performance management, and policy dissemination. Employees often faced delays in accessing critical HR information stored in SAP SuccessFactors.

Implementation

The company introduced a RAG solution integrated with its HR portal. The system was fine-tuned to retrieve policy documents, employee records, and training materials, while generating answers to frequently asked HR queries.

Steps taken:

1. **Knowledge Base Optimization**: Updating and structuring HR data for RAG integration.

2. **Multilingual Support**: Ensuring the system could handle queries in multiple languages.

3. **Interactive Portal**: Embedding the RAG-powered assistant into the HR portal for employee use.

Outcomes

Employee query resolution time decreased by 50%, and onboarding time was reduced by 30%. HR teams reported a 25% increase in productivity as routine queries were handled by the RAG system.

Lessons Learned

- RAG systems can offload routine tasks, allowing HR teams to focus on strategic initiatives.
- Multilingual capabilities improve accessibility for global workforces.
- Continuous updates to the knowledge base are essential for long-term success.

Case Study: Enhancing CRM Insights in Salesforce for a B2B Firm

Background

A B2B SaaS company struggled to extract meaningful insights from its Salesforce CRM, where customer interactions, sales data, and support tickets were stored. Sales teams faced challenges in identifying high-priority leads and crafting personalized outreach strategies.

Implementation

The firm integrated a RAG system with Salesforce to provide real-time retrieval of customer data, such as engagement history, product preferences, and support issues. The system also generated tailored sales strategies and email drafts based on retrieved information.

Steps included:

1. **Customer Data Cleaning**: Normalizing CRM data for accurate retrieval.

2. **AI Training**: Fine-tuning the RAG model with industry-specific customer scenarios.

3. **Sales Assistant Deployment**: Embedding the solution into the Salesforce dashboard.

Outcomes

The system increased lead conversion rates by 20% and reduced sales cycle times by 15%. Sales teams appreciated the ability to quickly retrieve relevant insights, leading to more effective client interactions.

Lessons Learned

- Integrating RAG with CRM systems drives higher personalization in sales efforts.

- Training the model with domain-specific data boosts its relevance and effectiveness.

- Real-time insights enable faster, more informed decision-making.

Case Study: Reducing Downtime in Manufacturing with RAG-Powered Predictive Maintenance

Background

A heavy machinery manufacturer faced frequent production downtimes due to delayed maintenance. Identifying the root cause of issues from a vast array of machine logs and manuals was time-consuming.

Implementation

The company deployed a RAG solution that combined historical maintenance records, IoT sensor data, and equipment manuals to generate predictive maintenance insights. The system was integrated with their existing maintenance management software.

Key steps:

1. **Data Integration**: Aggregating maintenance logs, manuals, and IoT data into a single system.

2. **Predictive Insights**: Training the RAG system to highlight patterns and recommend maintenance schedules.

3. **Field Application**: Providing technicians with mobile access to RAG-generated insights.

Outcomes

Unplanned downtime was reduced by 25%, and maintenance costs decreased by 15%. The system's ability to predict potential failures allowed the company to schedule proactive interventions, minimizing production disruptions.

Lessons Learned

- Combining RAG with IoT data creates powerful predictive capabilities.

- Mobile accessibility ensures insights are available where they're needed most.

- Regular updates to the model ensure it adapts to evolving operational patterns.

Case Study: Transforming Financial Analysis with RAG in an Investment Firm

Background

An investment firm needed a faster way to analyze financial reports, market news, and stock performance data to make real-time trading decisions. Traditional methods required analysts to manually sift through disparate sources, leading to delayed responses.

Implementation

The firm implemented a RAG system that retrieved financial reports, real-time market data, and news articles. The system also generated summaries and insights, including risk assessments and trend analyses.

Steps taken:

1. **Data Source Integration**: Connecting the RAG system to financial APIs, news platforms, and internal databases.

2. **Generative Analysis**: Training the system to generate actionable trading insights.

3. **Trader Support Tool**: Embedding RAG into the firm's trading platform.

Outcomes

The firm reported a 30% increase in trading efficiency and a 20% improvement in portfolio performance. Analysts were able to focus on strategy rather than data collection, significantly enhancing productivity.

Lessons Learned

- Real-time retrieval and generation are critical for fast-paced industries like finance.

- RAG systems excel in synthesizing information from multiple sources.

- Providing actionable insights adds value beyond simple data retrieval.

6. Conclusion: Unveiling a New Era of Enterprise Intelligence with RAG

Congratulations! You've embarked on a journey to unlock the transformative potential of Retrieval-Augmented Generation (RAG) for your enterprise applications. By following the steps outlined in this guide, you've laid the groundwork for a powerful system that empowers your workforce to leverage data like never before.

6.1 Benefits of a Successful RAG Deployment

A well-implemented RAG system offers a multitude of benefits for your organization:

- **Enhanced Decision-Making:** RAG equips your employees with faster access to insightful data, enabling them to make data-driven decisions with greater confidence.

- **Improved Efficiency and Productivity:** Streamlined workflows and automated tasks free up valuable time for your workforce to focus on higher-level strategic initiatives.

- **Deeper Data Analysis:** RAG unlocks a deeper understanding of your enterprise data, revealing trends and insights that might have otherwise gone unnoticed.

- **Increased User Satisfaction:** A user-friendly interface and accurate responses foster a positive user experience, encouraging wider adoption of RAG within your organization.

- **Competitive Advantage:** By leveraging the power of AI-driven data retrieval and generation, you position your enterprise at the forefront of innovation and efficiency.

The impact of a successful RAG deployment goes beyond mere data management. It fosters a culture of data-driven decision-making and empowers your workforce to become more informed, efficient, and productive.

6.2 Future of RAG in Enterprise Applications

The field of RAG is still in its early stages, but its potential is vast. Here's a glimpse into the future of RAG in enterprise applications:

- **Domain-Specific LLMs:** Expect to see a rise in LLMs pre-trained on specific industry domains, further enhancing the accuracy and relevance of

RAG outputs within your enterprise applications (e.g., healthcare-focused LLMs for medical record analysis).

- **Advanced Integration with Business Processes:** RAG will seamlessly integrate with various business processes, automating tasks and generating reports on a deeper level, further streamlining workflows across departments.

- **Enhanced Explainability and Transparency:** Future RAG systems will offer increased explainability, allowing users to understand the reasoning behind generated responses and fostering trust in the system's outputs.

As RAG technology continues to evolve, it holds the potential to revolutionize the way we interact with and utilize data within enterprise applications. By

embracing RAG now, you're positioning your

organization at the forefront of this exciting

technological shift.

Chapter: Integrating RAG into Enterprise Knowledge Management

In modern enterprises, knowledge is often scattered across systems, documents, and teams, making it difficult to access when needed. This chapter explores how Retrieval-Augmented Generation (RAG) systems can transform knowledge management by centralizing data retrieval and generating contextually relevant insights.

Key areas include:

- **Unifying Disparate Data Sources**: Leveraging RAG to retrieve information from internal databases, document repositories, and cloud-based systems.
- **Dynamic Knowledge Retrieval**: Providing employees with precise, real-time answers to complex queries.
- **Improved Collaboration**: Using RAG-generated summaries to facilitate cross-team communication and decision-making.
- **Automation of Knowledge Tasks**: Automatically generating FAQs, training guides, and best practice documents.
- **Case Study**: How a global enterprise reduced knowledge retrieval time by 50% using a RAG-enhanced system.

Chapter: RAG for Proactive IT Incident Management

Managing IT incidents in enterprise environments requires timely resolution to minimize operational disruptions. RAG systems can predict, retrieve, and address issues before they escalate. This chapter examines how enterprises can integrate RAG into IT service management (ITSM) platforms to enhance incident management.

Key discussion points:

- **Predictive Incident Resolution**: Using RAG to analyze logs and identify potential system failures.
- **Automated Troubleshooting**: Generating step-by-step resolutions based on retrieved knowledge base articles and system diagnostics.
- **Real-Time Reporting**: Creating automated incident summaries for stakeholders.
- **Integration with ITSM Tools**: Embedding RAG into platforms like ServiceNow and Jira.
- **Case Study**: Analyzing how a tech company reduced mean time to resolution (MTTR) by 30% with RAG.

Chapter: RAG-Driven Financial Forecasting and Planning

Financial forecasting and planning are critical to enterprise success, yet they are often hampered by fragmented data and complex analytics. This chapter explores how RAG systems enhance financial workflows by retrieving relevant data and generating accurate, actionable insights.

Highlights include:

- **Real-Time Data Aggregation**: Retrieving data from ERP systems, financial reports, and external market sources.
- **Generative Insights**: Producing financial models, budget scenarios, and risk analyses.
- **Dynamic Planning**: Enabling real-time updates to financial forecasts based on market changes.
- **Compliance Integration**: Ensuring all forecasts adhere to financial regulations.
- **Case Study**: How a multinational enterprise achieved 25% faster budget cycles with RAG-enhanced financial planning.

Case Study : Revolutionizing Customer Support in E-Commerce with RAG

Industry: E-Commerce

Challenge: A leading e-commerce platform faced challenges in scaling its customer support operations due to an overwhelming volume of inquiries. Agents struggled to retrieve accurate answers from a vast knowledge base spanning product catalogs, order histories, and customer service scripts.

Solution: The company integrated a RAG system into its customer support workflow. The system retrieved relevant information from internal knowledge bases, including product specifications, return policies, and FAQs, and generated contextually accurate responses. It was also integrated into the chatbot for first-line support.

Outcome:

- Reduced average resolution time by 40%.

- Increased customer satisfaction scores (CSAT) by 25%.

- Chatbots resolved 60% of queries without escalation to human agents.

- Employees reported greater efficiency and reduced frustration during complex cases.

Case Study : Enhancing Compliance in the Financial Sector with RAG

Industry: Banking and Financial Services

Challenge: A multinational bank struggled with monitoring and adhering to rapidly changing regulatory requirements across multiple countries. Compliance teams often spent weeks manually analyzing regulatory updates and implementing necessary changes.

Solution: The bank deployed a RAG system that retrieved regulatory updates from global databases, summarized them, and cross-referenced them with internal policies and processes. The system also generated actionable insights for compliance officers to prioritize tasks.

Outcome:

- Reduced time to implement compliance changes by 50%.
- Avoided regulatory fines due to missed updates.
- Enhanced the accuracy of compliance audits with automated reporting tools.

- Compliance team productivity increased by 30%.

Case Study : Streamlining Supply Chain Operations for a Manufacturing Giant

Industry: Manufacturing

Challenge: A global manufacturing company faced inefficiencies in its supply chain, including delays in supplier communication and inaccurate inventory forecasting, leading to production downtime.

Solution: The company implemented a RAG-based system that retrieved real-time data from supplier portals, logistics systems, and internal inventory records. It used this data to generate actionable forecasts and recommend adjustments to supply schedules.

Outcome:

- Reduced production downtime by 20%.

- Improved inventory forecasting accuracy by 35%.

- Achieved a 15% cost reduction in logistics operations through better planning.

- Enhanced supplier relationships due to improved communication.

Case Study : Optimizing Sales Operations with RAG in a SaaS Company

Industry: SaaS

Challenge: A SaaS company struggled to prioritize leads and personalize sales pitches due to fragmented customer data spread across CRM systems, emails, and third-party integrations.

Solution: The company integrated a RAG solution into its CRM, enabling sales teams to retrieve consolidated customer insights and generate tailored outreach strategies. The system also suggested optimal times to contact leads based on retrieved interaction data.

Outcome:

- Increased lead conversion rates by 28%.
- Reduced time spent on lead research by 40%.

- Personalized email campaigns resulted in a 20% higher engagement rate.

- Sales teams closed deals 15% faster on average.

Case Study : Improving Employee Training and Onboarding with RAG

Industry: Healthcare

Challenge: A hospital network needed to streamline its employee onboarding and training process. Staff members often found it challenging to locate specific procedural documents, training materials, and compliance requirements in a timely manner.

Solution: The hospital implemented a RAG system that retrieved and summarized relevant training materials, compliance policies, and procedural guides. It also generated personalized onboarding plans based on the roles of new hires.

Outcome:

- Reduced onboarding time by 25%.
- Increased employee satisfaction with training resources by 30%.
- Improved compliance adherence during the training phase.
- Reduced errors in early-stage employee performance due to better resource accessibility.